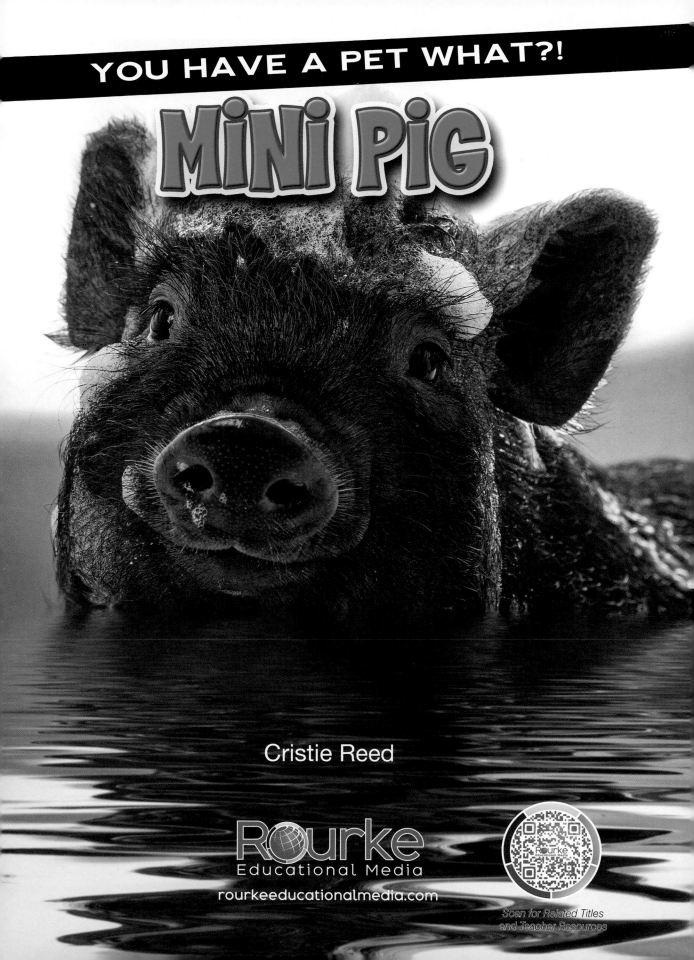

YOU HAVE A PET WHAT?!

MiNi PiG

Cristie Reed

Rourke
Educational Media

rourkeeducationalmedia.com

Before Reading:

Building Academic Vocabulary and Background Knowledge

Before reading a book, it is important to tap into what your child or students already know about the topic. This will help them develop their vocabulary, increase their reading comprehension, and make connections across the curriculum.

1. *Look at the cover of the book. What will this book be about?*
2. *What do you already know about the topic?*
3. *Let's study the Table of Contents. What will you learn about in the book's chapters?*
4. *What would you like to learn about this topic? Do you think you might learn about it from this book? Why or why not?*
5. *Use a reading journal to write about your knowledge of this topic. Record what you already know about the topic and what you hope to learn about the topic.*
6. *Read the book.*
7. *In your reading journal, record what you learned about the topic and your response to the book.*
8. *After reading the book complete the activities below.*

Content Area Vocabulary
Read the list. What do these words mean?

breed
domestic
exotic
graze
nature
neutered
positive reinforcement
rooting
sanctuary
social
spayed
swine
temperament

After Reading:

Comprehension and Extension Activity

After reading the book, work on the following questions with your child or students in order to check their level of reading comprehension and content mastery.

1. *Would a mini pig be a good fit in your home? Explain. (Text to self connection)*
2. *Why were mini pigs bred? (Summarize)*
3. *Why is it important to keep cords and plastic bags off the floor if you have a pet mini pig? (Asking questions)*
4. *When purchasing a mini pig, what should you look for? (Summarize)*
5. *Why does a pig roll in mud? (Asking questions)*

Extension Activity
Are mini pigs good pets? Using the book, create a T-chart with reasons why mini pigs are good pets and reasons why they are not good pets. Choose a side and write an opinion paper with supporting reasons from your T-chart. You can extend on your reasons by finding additional information found on reliable Internet sources. Share you opinion paper with your classmates, teachers, or parents.

Table of Contents

Meet the Mini

When you come home to a dog or cat you are greeted by barks, meows, and wagging tails. Keep the wagging tails and substitute snorts, grunts, or squeals – that is the happy greeting you receive when you come home to a mini pig.

Miniature, potbellied, micro, pocket, and teacup are names for a type of dwarf **swine** bred to be smaller than a **domestic** farm pig. Their good **temperament** and small size have made them popular pets in North America and Europe.

▶▶ *Pigs are fast learners. A scientist once taught pigs to play video games!*

Mini piglets come into the world no bigger than a kitten. They grow quickly. An adult may weigh about 100 pounds (45 kilograms). They stand about 18 inches (45 centimeters) high at the shoulder. Depending on the **breed** and the size of their parents, they may grow larger or smaller. Their typical lifespan is 10 to 15 years. Some mini pig breeds can live longer.

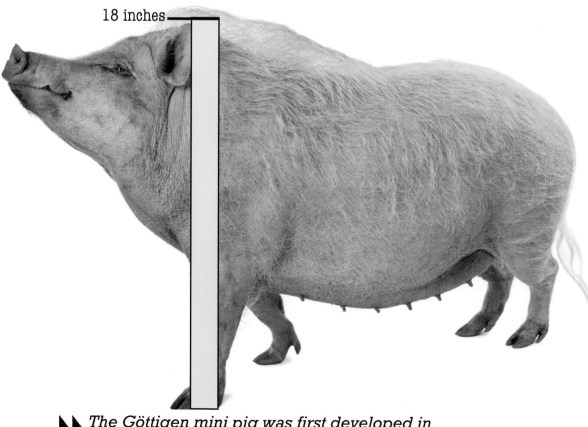

18 inches

 The Göttigen mini pig was first developed in Europe for medical research.

Just like farm pigs, mini pigs are known for their chubby round bodies, flat noses, and curly tails. Their large ears stand up straight and their small, dark eyes are protected by long lashes. They have thick, strong snouts for **rooting** and digging. On each foot they have a hoof. Their tails can be curly, straight, or kinked.

Mini pigs have some distinctive characteristics. They will never grow as large as a typical farm pig. They may have a swayed back and an oversized belly that makes them look like they've eaten too much. Their legs are usually short, which makes their bellies nearly touch the ground.

FUN FACT

Pigs are cloven-hoofed, which means their hoof is split into two toes. They walk on two front toes and have two back toes called dewclaws.

Many Breeds of Mini Pigs

Mini Pig Breeds	Adult Weight	Color	Unique Characteristics	Photo
Vietnamese potbellied pig or potbellied pig	90-150 pounds (40-68 kilograms)	solid black, white, or a mix of both	swayed back, potbelly, wrinkled skin, short turned up nose, straight tail	
Guinea hog or African pygmy	100-300 pounds (45-135 kilograms)	black	straight back, short legs, short snout, kinky tail, bristly coat	
Ossabaw Island pig or feral pigs	40-90 pounds (18-40 kilograms)	solid gray, blue, or red; spotted black and white, calico	straight back and belly, long snout, medium ears, heavy coat	
Juliana pig or painted miniature	50 pounds (22 kilograms)	solid red, black, silver, white, or a mix of two colors	longer legs, slight potbelly, small ears, straight tail	
Göttigen	50-100 pounds (22-45 kilograms)	pink and black	straight back and belly, sparse hair, short snout, medium ears	
Kunekune	70 pounds (31 kilograms)	solid black, gold, tan, brown, or black and white	straight back, rounded belly, short legs, short upturned nose, curly tail, tassels that hang from lower jaw	

Once Upon A Time

Mini pigs have existed on different continents around the world for hundreds of years. Ancestors of mini pigs were brought to North America by early settlers as a source of food. In Europe, mini pigs were bred for medical research before they became popular as pets.

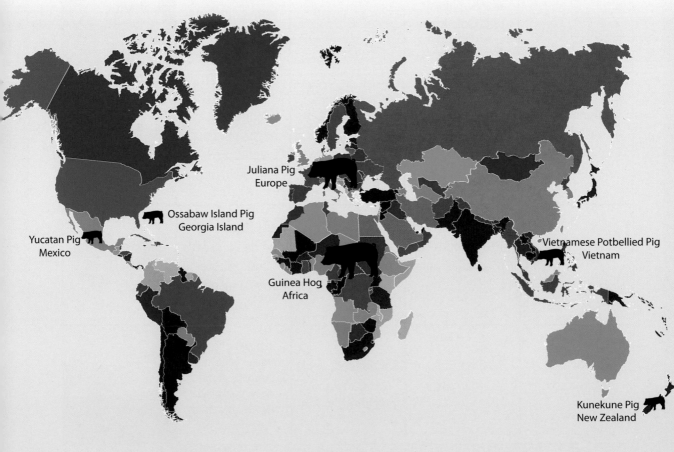

Juliana Pig
Europe

Ossabaw Island Pig
Georgia Island

Yucatan Pig
Mexico

Vietnamese Potbellied Pig
Vietnam

Guinea Hog
Africa

Kunekune Pig
New Zealand

Vietnamese potbellied pigs were imported to North America by a Canadian zookeeper in the 1980s. That specific group of pigs was bred and their offspring were sent to zoos in the United States. When people saw them, they quickly fell in love with the petite pigs. They thought they might make great pets. More attention came to mini pigs when wealthy people and celebrities began purchasing them. The popularity of these **exotic** pigs spread rapidly in the 1980s.

 A young woman and her pet pig pose for a photo in the 1920s.

Going Whole Hog

Mini pigs have unique personalities. They can be quirky and lovable, but sometimes stubborn or pig-headed. They are extremely curious and very intelligent. They use their squeals, snorts, and grunts to show happiness and communicate their needs. When they want something, you will hear about it!

▶▶ *Pigs have excellent memories.*

It is in the pig's **nature** to use its thick, strong snout to root and dig. Wallowing on their backs and scratching with their hooves is also normal pig behavior. Pigs love to eat. Some clever pigs have learned to open refrigerators and cupboards to get a treat!

You can find tips and tricks for training your mini pig on the Internet.

Pigs are **social** animals. Mini pigs like lots of attention and enjoy the companionship of their humans and other pigs. They develop a strong and trusting bond with their owners. They run, jump, and play with children and other pets.

They like to give and receive affection. Mini pigs snuggle with their humans on the couch or curl up with them in bed. They are in hog heaven when they get a back rub or a belly scratch. They love a good bath.

A Pig-tionary

boar: a male pig

hog: a larger pig

litter: a group of piglets born to a sow

pettitoes: a tiny pig's feet

pig: common term for a younger animal

piggy: a sow late in her pregnancy

piggery: a place where pigs are kept

piglet: a baby pig from birth to eight weeks of age

runt: the smallest piglet in a litter

sow: a female pig

This Little Piggy

Mini piglets need to stay with their mother until they are eight weeks old. When they arrive in the home as pets, they need their own space. They will naturally be frightened and need time to get used to their new environment. Provide an area separate from humans and other pets. The piglet needs to feel safe and secure. This is how it can start to develop trust with its new family members.

▶▶ *A dog or cat bed will also work well for your mini pig.*

To become a good pet, proper socialization is critical. It takes love, patience, and time to get to know your new pet. Gradually introduce yourself and other family members to the young pig. Some piglets are not fond of being picked up or held. They use their high-pitched squeal to let you know when they are afraid.

FUN FACT

Piglets are among the noisiest of all babies! Their squeals can reach 115 decibels. That's as loud as a rock concert!

Everything's Piggy!

The mini piglet needs a pen with a bed in its new home. A playpen works well. Provide lots of blankets and towels for rooting and burrowing. They enjoy having a few soft toys to push around with their snouts. Mini piglets need special baby food and plenty of water for drinking. Put a litter box in their pen. They can start to use it right away.

As the piglet grows, it will need to go outdoors. It needs plenty of exercise and walks, just like a dog. A fenced yard allows the mini pig to safely play, rest, and **graze** outside. It needs a covered area for shade and protection from the Sun. Their rest area should have fresh hay for napping and

snacking. During warmer weather, a kiddie pool is a great place for pigs to cool off, splash, and make mud.

Pet Pointers

White or light-colored pigs fare better in warm, sunny climates. Dark-colored pigs fare better in cooler, less sunny climates.

Indoor pigs need a safe space that is pig-proof. Set up gates to keep the mini pig contained in its area. Keep dangerous objects such as cords and plastic bags off the floor. Cover slick floors with cloth or rugs.

Pet Pointers

One of the benefits of owning a mini pig is that they don't shed. They have hair, not fur. This makes them good pets for people with pet allergies. Another benefit is that they seldom get fleas.

Mini pigs must be fed a high-quality pig chow to get protein and important nutrients. They need fresh raw vegetables such as potatoes, carrots, and lettuce. Find out how much food is right and set up a feeding schedule. Be careful of overfeeding a mini pig because it could gain too much weight.

As Happy as a Pig in Mud!

Pigs have an undeserved reputation for being filthy animals. But their slovenliness can be attributed to the fact that they have no sweat glands and they are easily sunburned. They roll in mud to cool off and protect themselves from the Sun.

A dip in mud can lower a pig's temperature by 3.6 degrees Fahrenheit (2 degrees Celsius).

When Pigs Fly!

We will never actually see a pig fly, but they can learn to do some amazing feats. Mini pigs are very trainable and have good memories. Mini pigs can learn to ride skateboards, run in races, and jump through hoops. They learn their names very quickly and respond well to commands such as "Come" or "Sit."

▶▶ *Mini pig races are popular at many fairs and festivals.*

Mini pigs learn best with **positive reinforcement**. Pigs love to eat, so training treats, such as fruit, make great rewards for correct behavior. They also respond to the tone of your voice and affection. Never use force with a mini pig. Just like dogs and cats, mini pigs can be housebroken or potty trained. They can be taught to walk on a leash and can travel in the car.

▶▶ *After you've bonded with your pet, you can teach it all kinds of tricks.*

Responsible Mini Pig Ownership

When considering mini pig ownership, look for a caring and knowledgeable mini pig breeder. Try to see the mini pig's parents to determine the pig's eventual size and overall well-being.

Pet Pointers

The cost of a mini pig can range from $800 to $1,000 or more.

Look for a good temperament. The mini pig should be active and energetic. It should not be too fat. It should have clear eyes and straight, clean teeth. Their hooves should be trimmed and free from damage.

A specially qualified veterinarian is necessary to keep mini pigs healthy and provide proper medical care. Mini pigs must be **spayed** or **neutered** to be good pets. Females should be spayed to prevent unwanted litters of piglets. Unneutered male pigs give off a bad smell and can become aggressive. Males should be neutered by eight weeks of age and females should be spayed at 12 weeks.

▶▶ *A pet mini should have a check-up with a veterinarian at least once a year.*

Before purchasing a mini piglet, consider adopting a mini pig from a pig rescue center. These organizations provide a **sanctuary** for unwanted mini pigs and help find new homes for them. There are many pig rescue organizations across the United States. Future mini pig owners can visit and volunteer at rescue sites to learn more about mini pig ownership and care.

ADOPT
A
MINI PIG

Owning a mini pig is not legal in all neighborhoods and communities. Zoning laws for mini pigs are different from state to state and from city to city. In some places, mini pigs are considered livestock and they cannot be kept in any area where livestock is not permitted. Contact the zoning department of the city or county where you live to see if zoning laws permit mini pig ownership. If you have a homeowner's association you will also have to check with them. If you are a renter, you need to be sure your lease allows for exotic pets.

Things to Think About If You Want a Pet Mini Pig

- Do the zoning laws in your area allow you to own one?

- Mini pigs can spend some of their time indoors. They also need time outdoors with enough space to run, play, graze, and relieve themselves. Their outdoor area should have a place to rest, a fence, and shade for protection from the Sun.

- Mini pigs need health care from a veterinarian that is specially trained to work with farm animals. They need vaccinations and their hooves and teeth need regular care. A mini pig will need to be spayed or neutered in order to be a good pet.

- Mini pigs like to root and dig. These behaviors can cause damage to indoor and outdoor areas. Your house and yard need to be safe and able to withstand a strong, active animal.

- When you see a mini piglet, be aware that the tiny creature will grow to a much larger size.

- Mini pigs live for 15 years or more. Owning one is a long-term commitment.

- Mini pigs are social animals. They don't like to be left alone for long periods of time. When they get bored they may become destructive.

- Mini pigs need to be fed a special diet to stay healthy.

- Mini pigs need lots of time, training, and attention.

- It's important to consider if a mini pig will fit in with other pets in the household.

Glossary

breed (breed): a particular type of animal

domestic (duh-MESS-tic): animals kept at home for work, food, or as pets

exotic (eg-ZOT-ik): strange or unusual; from a faraway country

graze (graz): eating grass

nature (NAY-chur): the character of something or someone

neutered (NOO-turd): to have had a medical procedure that prevents male animals from reproducing

positive reinforcement (POZ-uh-tiv ree-in-FORSS-muhnt): a reward given to strengthen behavior

rooting (ROOT-ing): to dig or push through soil

sanctuary (SANGK-choo-er-ee): an area where animals are protected

social (SOH-shuhl): animals that live in groups and enjoy being around others

spayed (spayd): to have had a medical procedure that prevents female animals from reproducing

swine (swin): a type of mammal from the family Suidae

temperament (TEM-pur-uh-muhnt): personality; the way an animal thinks, acts, or responds to others

Index

Show What You Know

1. Explain both the challenges and benefits of having a mini pig for a pet.

2. Describe the similarities and differences between having a mini pig for a pet and having a dog for a pet.

3. When did mini pigs become popular pets?

4. What is the average lifespan of a pet mini pig?

5. What are some things you must do to prepare before purchasing a mini pig?

Websites to Visit

www.pbskids.org/itsmylife/family/pets/article7.html

www.dogonews.com/2009/10/8/teacup-piglets

www.pigs4ever.com

About the Author

Cristie Reed is a literacy teacher and lifelong animal lover. She grew up on a small farm in southern Indiana and experienced the joys of owning many amazing pets. In her lifetime she has owned and cared for three pet goats, a few chickens, a few ducks, a green snake, two anole lizards, a guinea pig, a Shetland pony, a caiman, a squirrel, three cats, eight dogs, and one very special peacock. She currently lives in Florida with her husband and miniature schnauzer, Rocky.

Meet The Author!
www.meetREMauthors.com

© 2016 Rourke Educational Media

www.rourkeeducationalmedia.com

PHOTO CREDITS: Cover: ©Rhea Magaro; page 1, page 18 (top), page 24 (left), page 25: ©Kuttelvaserova Stuchelova; page 3, page 9 (d): ©JIANG HONGYAN; page 5: ©Nicole Hollenstein; page 6, page 9 (e): ©Lifeonwhite; page 7: ©Shenki; page 8, page 15, page 23 (left): ©Rita Kochmarjova; page 9 (a): ©Goldika; page 9 (b): ©Dennis van deWater; page 9 (c): ©Michaela Stejskalova; page 9 (f): ©LazingBee; page 11: ©Everett Collection; page 12, page 19 (left), page 20(bottom): ©ADogsLifePhotography; page 13: ©Tamaz Levstek; page 14: ©WooodenDinosaur; page 16: ©Kuban_girl; page 17: ©SchulteProductions; page 18 (bottom): ©33333; page 19 (right): ©Farinosa; page 20 (top): ©Kitch Bain; page 21 ©jadimages; page 22: ©GoldenCreations; page 23 (right): ©Patrick Heagney; page 24 (right), page 27: ©iLexx; page 26: ©Alan Poulson; page 28: ©Steven van Soldt; page 30: ©notelaurens

Edited by: Keli Sipperley

Cover design and Interior design by: Rhea Magaro

Library of Congress PCN Data

Mini Pig/Cristie Reed
(You Have a Pet What?!)
  ISBN 978-1-63430-431-3 (hard cover)
  ISBN 978-1-63430-531-0 (soft cover)
  ISBN 978-1-63430-620-1 (e-Book)
Library of Congress Control Number: 2015931851

Printed in the United States of America, North Mankato, Minnesota

Also Available as: